PROMISE
AND DELIVERANCE
BIBLE CURRICULUM

Level 1

Harvey De Groot

Edited by Norlan De Groot
Illustrations and Activities by D.A. Dawal

All Scripture quotations, unless otherwise indicated, are taken from the New King James Version. Copyright © 1982 by Thomas Nelson.

Lesson text copyright © 2024 by Harvey De Groot, Norlan De Groot.
Illustrations and activities copyright © 2024 by D. A. Dawal.

CONTENTS

Lesson	Page
Preface	5
1. The Kingdom of God (Genesis 1:1–2:3)	7
2. The Covenant of God's Favor (Genesis 2:4-25)	29
3. The Covenant of God's Grace (Genesis 3)	41
4. Living Seed (Genesis 4)	53
5. Saved by Water (Genesis 6–9)	65
6. The Emergence of Distinct Peoples (Genesis 11:1-9)	79
7. Blessed in the One (Genesis 12)	91
8. Christ Alone (Genesis 13)	103
9. Blessed by the Greater (Genesis 14)	115
10. The Lord in the Covenant (Genesis 15)	127
11. God Hears (Genesis 16)	139
12. God the Almighty (Genesis 17)	151
Answer Keys	163

PREFACE

When S.G. De Graaf wrote his four-volume series, *Promise and Deliverance*, he showed educators how to teach Bible stories from a redemptive-historical perspective. Rather than turning Bible stories into moralistic tales, De Graaf taught us how all the Bible shows God revealing himself as the God of the covenant, who is working out His redemptive plan for humanity and all of creation.

The Bible curriculum found in this book supplements De Graaf's work. The lessons are divided into twenty volumes with four levels per volume. The four levels allow families with students in various grades to study Bible stories together. The levels are divided according to the following grades:

> Level One: Grades K-1
> Level Two: Grades 2-3
> Level Three: Grades 4-6
> Level Four: Grades 7-8

De Graaf wrote his series for teachers. He intended teachers to study his lessons prior to teaching a class. The curriculum in this book has a different purpose. It is designed for teachers to use with the students in class. It is appropriate for use in Sunday Schools, homeschools, Christian day schools, and any other place where systematic instruction in the Bible is desired.

The 12 lessons in this Bible curriculum correspond to the following lessons in De Graaf's series:

Bible Curriculum	De Graaf's Series
Volume 1, Lesson 1	Volume 1, Lesson 1
Volume 1, Lesson 2	Volume 1, Lesson 2
Volume 1, Lesson 3	Volume 1, Lesson 3
Volume 1, Lesson 4	Volume 1, Lesson 4
Volume 1, Lesson 5	Volume 1, Lesson 5
Volume 1, Lesson 6	Volume 1, Lesson 6
Volume 1, Lesson 7	Volume 1, Lesson 7
Volume 1, Lesson 8	Volume 1, Lesson 8
Volume 1, Lesson 9	Volume 1, Lesson 9
Volume 1, Lesson 10	Volume 1, Lesson 10
Volume 1, Lesson 11	Volume 1, Lesson 11
Volume 1, Lesson 12	Volume 1, Lesson 12

The lessons you will find in this Bible curriculum were written by Harvey De Groot and were edited by his son Norlan De Groot. The Teaching Aids (T.A.), both illustrations and activities, were created by D.A. Dawal.

THE KINGDOM OF GOD

LESSON 1

Scripture: Genesis 1:1–2:3

Memory Verse: "All things were made through Him." (John 1:3a)

Lesson Truth: God made all things.

LESSON

God made all the things we can see. God made the sun and moon and stars. He made all the trees and flowers. He made all the animals and people. God made all things in six normal days. He made all things out of nothing. He just said, "Let there be . . ." and there they were.

The first day God made day and God made night. (Show T.A. 1.1)
The second day God made the sky and the air. (Show T.A. 1.2)
The third day God made the oceans, the lakes, and the mountains. (Show T.A. 1.3)

The fourth day God made the sun to shine each day. He made the moon and stars to shine each night. (Show T.A. 1.4)
The fifth day God made all the fish and all the birds. (Show T.A. 1.5)
The sixth day God made all the animals. (Show T.A. 1.6)
Last of all, God made the first man and woman. (Show T.A. 1.6)

God made all these things in six days. Do you know what God did then? He rested. God wants you to rest each Sunday. He wants you to remember what He did, after He made all things.

Note to the teacher: *The acronym T.A. refers to Teaching Aid, which you can find in the Teaching Aids and Activities section.*

REVIEW QUESTIONS

Read these sentences to the students and ask them to say the correct answer.

1. Say YES to the things that God made:

Trees	Man	Birds	Moon
Animals	Fish	Sun	Stars

2. It took God (many years - a few weeks - six days) to make all things.

3. God made all things by (shouting - speaking).

4. On the seventh day God (worked - rested).

ACTIVITIES

To recap this lesson, do Activity 1.1. In case you still have enough time in your class, do Activities 1.2 and 1.3.

TEACHING AIDS & ACTIVITIES

These teaching aids and activities are designed to help you convey and review the Lesson. If you need to scan and reprint any activity sheet for your class, cut along these cutting lines.

"Then God said, 'Let there be light'; and there was light. And God saw the light, that it was good; and God divided the light from the darkness. God called the light Day, and the darkness He called Night. So the evening and the morning were the first day."

Genesis 1:3-5

TEACHING AID 1.1

On Day 1, God made the day and night.

"Then God said, 'Let there be a firmament in the midst of the waters, and let it divide the waters from the waters.' Thus God made the firmament, and divided the waters which were under the firmament from the waters which were above the firmament; and it was so. And God called the firmament Heaven. So the evening and the morning were the second day."

Genesis 1:6-8

TEACHING AID 1.2

On Day 2, God made the sky and the air.

"Then God said, 'Let the waters under the heavens be gathered together into one place, and let the dry land appear'; and it was so. And God called the dry land Earth, and the gathering together of the waters He called Seas...'"

"Then God said, 'Let the earth bring forth grass, the herb that yields seed, and the fruit tree that yields fruit according to its kind, whose seed is in itself, on the earth'; and it was so... So the evening and the morning were the third day."

Genesis 1:9-11,13

TEACHING AID 1.3

On Day 3, God made the oceans, lakes, land, trees, and plants.

"Then God made two great lights: the greater light to rule the day, and the lesser light to rule the night. He made the stars also. God set them in the firmament of the heavens to give light on the earth, and to rule over the day and over the night, and to divide the light from the darkness. And God saw that it was good. So the evening and the morning were the fourth day."

Genesis 1:16-19

TEACHING AID 1.4

On Day 4, God made the sun, moon, and stars.

"So God created great sea creatures and every living thing that moves, with which the waters abounded, according to their kind, and every winged bird according to its kind. And God saw that it was good. And God blessed them, saying, 'Be fruitful and multiply, and fill the waters in the seas, and let birds multiply on the earth.' So the evening and the morning were the fifth day."

Genesis 1:21-23

TEACHING AID 1.5

On Day 5, God made all the fish and all the birds.

"And God made the beast of the earth according to its kind, cattle according to its kind, and everything that creeps on the earth according to its kind. And God saw that it was good.
Then God said, 'Let Us make man in Our image, according to Our likeness...' So God created man in His own image; in the image of God He created him; male and female He created them."

Genesis 1:25-27

TEACHING AID 1.6

On Day 6, God made all the land animals, and the first man and woman.

ACTIVITY 1.1

Each of these boxes represents a day in creation. In each box, draw something God created.

DAY 3	DAY 4
DAY 5	DAY 6

✂ Cut here to detach this activity.

23

ACTIVITY 1.2

Circle all the creatures God made on Day 5.

Eagle

Lakes

Adam

Pumpkin

Angels

Goldfish

Hippo

Birch

Whale Shark

Oak

Lion

Hen

Blue Jay

Scorpion

Earthworm

Eve

ACTIVITY 1.3
Color this picture.

THE COVENANT OF GOD'S FAVOR

LESSON 2

Scripture: Genesis 2:4-25

Memory Verse: "And He will show them His covenant." (Psalm 25:14b)

Lesson Truth: God told the man and woman they could be His special friends.

LESSON

God made a beautiful garden. God said Adam and Eve could live in His beautiful garden. God wanted Adam and Eve to take care of His beautiful garden. God told Adam and Eve they could eat the fruit from all the trees in the garden except one in the middle of the garden. God said Adam and Eve would be His special friends if they would obey Him.

How sad it is that Adam and Eve did not obey God. They ate some of the fruit from the tree in the middle of the garden (Show T.A. 2.1). Now Adam and Eve could no longer live in God's beautiful garden and be His special friends. Will Adam and Eve ever be special friends of God again?

Yes, God made a way for Adam and Eve to be His friends again. Adam and Eve did not obey God. But our Lord Jesus Christ did obey God. So, Adam and Eve could once again be God's friends. Because Jesus did obey God, you and I can also be God's friends. We will tell about that friendship next time.

REVIEW QUESTIONS

Read these sentences to the students and ask them to say the correct answer.

1. Adam and Eve lived in a beautiful (house - garden).

2. Adam and Eve were told not to eat fruit from one tree (in the middle - at the end) of the garden.

3. Adam and Eve (obeyed - disobeyed) God and broke a special friendship with God.

4. Our Lord Jesus (obeyed - disobeyed) God so we can again have a special friendship with God.

ACTIVITIES

To recap this lesson, do Activity 2.1. In case you still have enough time in your class, do Activities 2.2 and 2.3.

TEACHING AIDS & ACTIVITIES

These teaching aids and activities are designed to help you convey and review the Lesson. If you need to scan and reprint any activity sheet for your class, cut along these cutting lines.

"And out of the ground the Lord God made every tree grow that is pleasant to the sight and good for food. The tree of life was also in the midst of the garden, and the tree of the knowledge of good and evil."

Genesis 2:9

TEACHING AID 2.1

Adam and Eve did not obey God.

33

ACTIVITY 2.1

Read Genesis 2:15-17. Fill in the blanks to know what God assigned to Adam and what He told him about the trees in the Garden.

"Then the _____ ___ took the man and ____ ____ in the _____ of _____ to _____ and _____ it. And the Lord God _____ the man, saying, 'Of _____ ____ of the _____ you may _____ eat; but of ____ _____ of the _____ of _____ and _____ you shall ____ ____, for in ____ ____ that you ____ of it ____ ____ _____ ____.'"

Note to teacher: *For this activity, please use the New King James Version.*

ACTIVITY 2.2

Answer these six sentences by writing the missing words on the blanks and on the squares below. Identify the word formed through the shaded squares to complete this sentence:

God placed Adam and Eve in the _____ of Eden.

1. _____ made the heavens and the earth.

2. God wanted _____ and Eve to take care of His beautiful garden.

3. God said Adam and Eve would be His special _____ if they would obey Him.

4. Adam and Eve could eat the fruit from all the trees in the garden except one in the _____ of the garden.

5. Sadly, Adam and _____ did not obey God.

6. Because Jesus obeyed God, Adam and Eve could once _____ be God's friends.

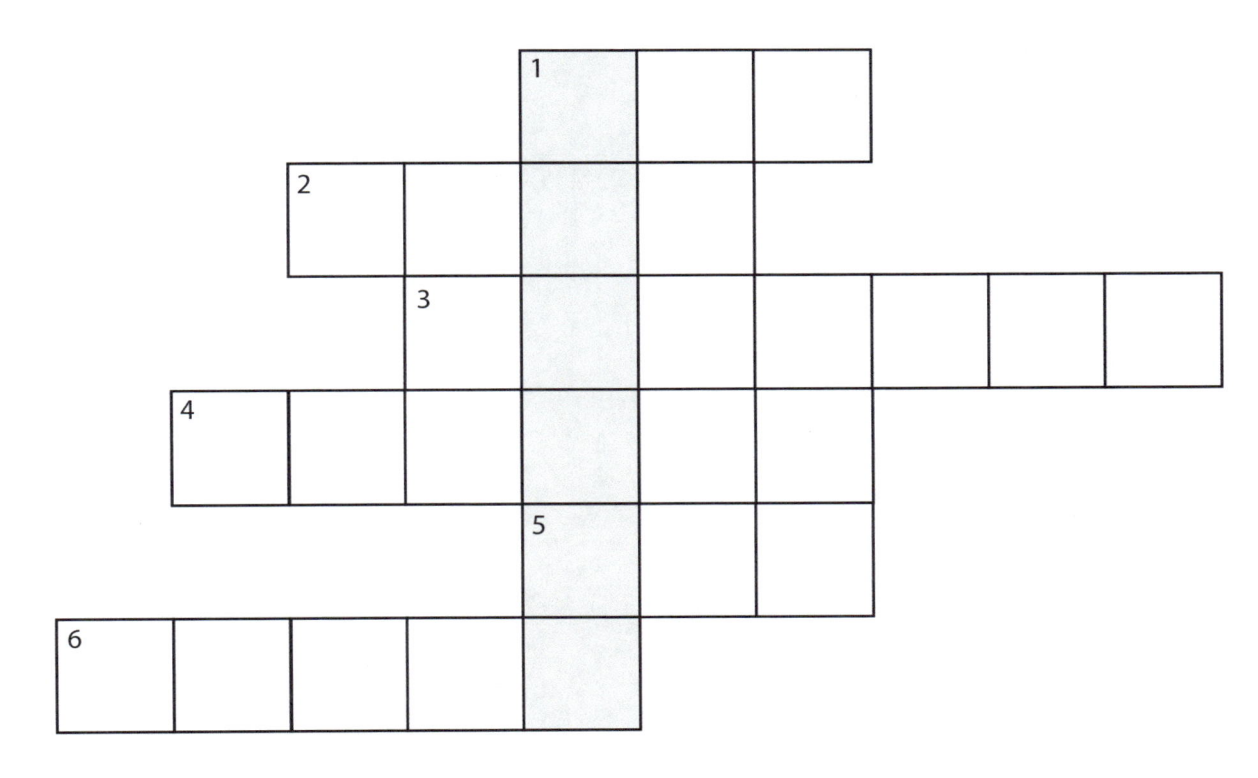

ACTIVITY 2.3
Color this picture.

THE COVENANT OF GOD'S GRACE

LESSON 3

Scripture: Genesis 3

Memory Verse: "I have made a covenant with my chosen." (Psalm 89:3a)

Lesson Truth: God told Adam and Eve about a new promise, after they had disobeyed Him in the Garden of Eden.

LESSON

Our Bible story today is about two actions. These two actions took place in the Garden of Eden. One action was done by Adam and Eve when they ate the fruit from the tree from which God had said they should not eat. The second action was done by God when He decided to give Adam and Eve a new promise. Even after they had disobeyed God, He still loved them.

What a sad story that God's enemy, Satan, came to talk to Adam and Eve. He made them believe it wasn't fair not to eat from the tree in the middle of the garden. Satan even lied to Adam and Eve about God's Word. He told Adam and Eve you will not surely die, as God has said if you eat the fruit from the tree. Satan made it seem so nice. He said you will not die, but your eyes will be opened. And if your eyes are opened you will know what is good and what is evil.

Then Adam and Eve ate the fruit from the tree. They disobeyed God. After they disobeyed God, they felt terrible. They were afraid of God and tried to hide from God. But God still loved them.

LESSON (Continued)

God loved Adam and Eve so much. Even after they disobeyed God, He promised them that one of Eve's great grandchildren would one day destroy Satan. God sent Adam and Eve out of the garden because they disobeyed. They could no longer live close to God in the garden. Instead they believed God's promise that Satan would be destroyed. The great grandchild of Eve who will destroy Satan is our Lord Jesus.

REVIEW QUESTIONS

Read these questions to the students and ask them to say the correct answer.

1. Who came and told Adam and Eve a lie about God's Word?

2. What did Adam and Eve do after they disobeyed God?

3. What did God promise would happen to Satan?

4. Who is the great grandchild of Eve who will destroy Satan?

ACTIVITIES

To recap this lesson, do Activity 3.1. In case you still have enough time in your class, do Activities 3.2 and 3.3.

TEACHING AIDS & ACTIVITIES

These teaching aids and activities are designed to help you convey and review the Lesson. If you need to scan and reprint any activity sheet for your class, cut along these cutting lines.

"And I will put enmity
Between you and the woman,
And between your seed and her Seed;
He shall bruise your head,
And you shall bruise His heel."

Genesis 3:15

TEACHING AID 3.1

Adam and Eve tried to hide from God.

ACTIVITY 3.1
Color this picture.

47

ACTIVITY 3.2

Solve this maze to help Adam and Eve find their new home outside the Garden of Eden.

ACTIVITY 3.3

Color the letters below. Write each letter on the box that matches its assigned number to reveal what God gave to Adam and Eve after they sinned.

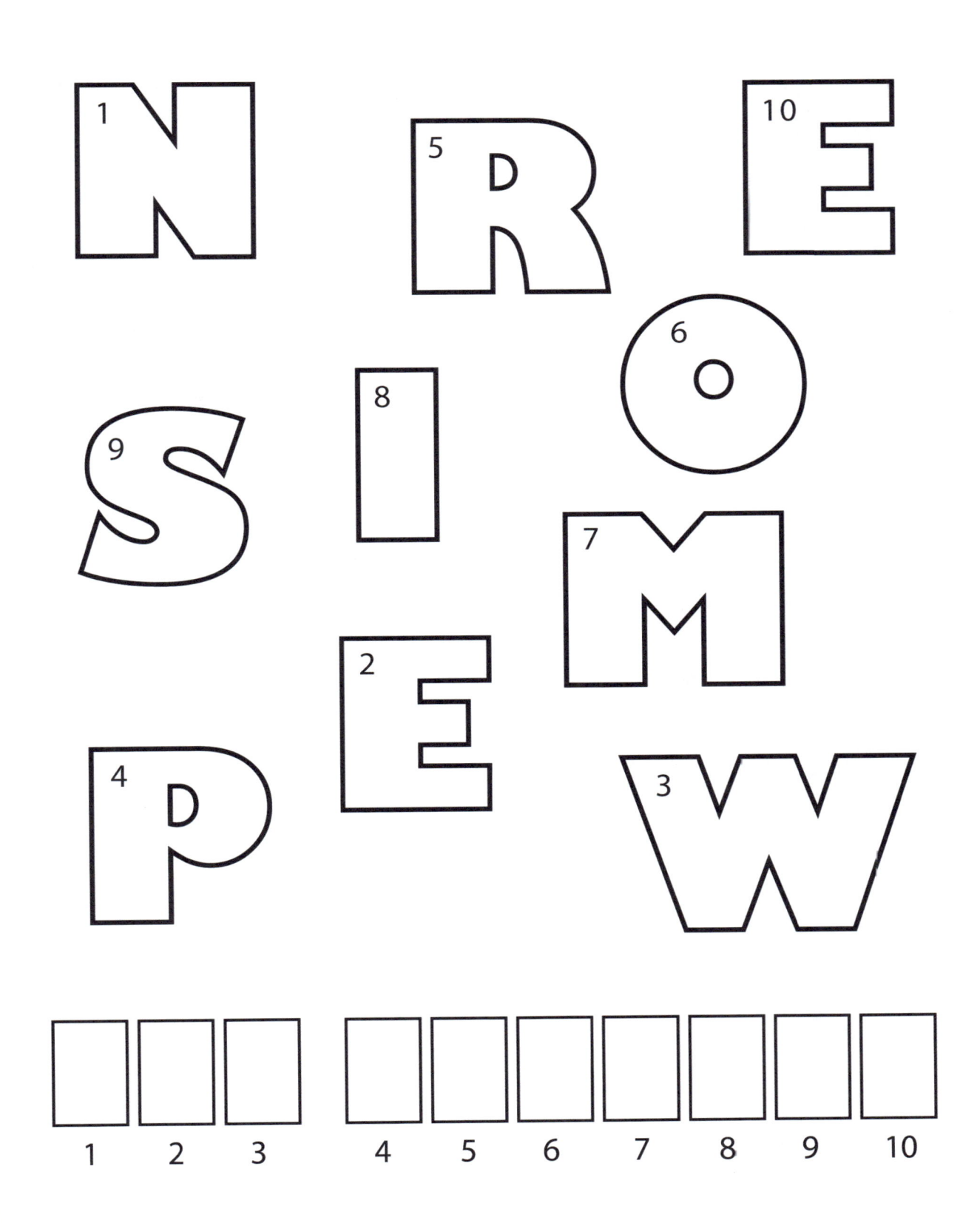

1	2	3	4	5	6	7	8	9	10

LIVING SEED

LESSON 4

Scripture: Genesis 4

Memory Verse: "For God has appointed another seed for me instead of Abel." (Genesis 4:25b)

Lesson Truth: God promised Adam and Eve that a son, who would follow them, would one day destroy Satan.

LESSON

When you make a promise to your little friends, do you always keep your promises? Sometimes we break our promises, but God never does. Today we are going to learn about our promise-keeping God. He kept His promises even when one of Adam and Eve's sons did a very a wicked thing.

Adam and Eve were sent out of God's beautiful garden. They were sent out of the garden because they disobeyed God. Think how happy they must have been when God gave them two little boys. They knew that God was keeping His promise. God had promised they would have children even outside the garden. Adam and Eve loved their little boys. They named them Cain and Abel. They taught them to worship God. They taught them to bring sacrifices to God.

One day Cain and Abel each brought a sacrifice to God. Abel had a heart that loved God, so God liked his sacrifice (Show T.A. 4.1). Cain did not have a heart that loved God, so God did not like his sacrifice.

LESSON (Continued)

Cain was angry because God did not like his sacrifice. He was angry at God and his brother Abel. Because he was angry Cain killed his brother Abel. Think how sad Adam and Eve must have been. Their son Cain was very wicked. Their son Abel was dead. How could God keep His promise if they did not have a son who loved God?

Remember God keeps His promises. God gave Adam and Eve another little boy. They named this boy, Seth. They named him, Seth, because they knew God had given them another son who loved God. Their son, Seth, would take the place of Abel, who was killed by Cain. God did keep His promise. He kept His promise to Adam and Eve. He gave them a son who loved God. He gave children to Seth who also loved God. One of these children from Seth would one day destroy Satan.

REVIEW QUESTIONS

Read these questions to the students and ask them to say the correct answer.

1. Who was Adam and Eve's son who did not love God? Cain - Abel - Seth

2. Who were the two sons who did love God? Cain - Abel - Seth

3. This story tells us about: Cain who was faithful? or God who is faithful?

4. The son of Adam and Eve and the son of Seth who will destroy Satan is: Abel - Jesus - Lamech

ACTIVITIES

To recap this lesson, do Activity 4.1. In case you still have enough time in your class, do Activities 4.2 and 4.3.

TEACHING AIDS & ACTIVITIES

These teaching aids and activities are designed to help you convey and review the Lesson. If you need to scan and reprint any activity sheet for your class, cut along these cutting lines.

"Abel also brought of the firstborn of his flock and of their fat. And the Lord respected Abel and his offering..."

Genesis 4:4

TEACHING AID 4.1

Abel had a heart that loved God. His sacrifice was pleasing to Him.

ACTIVITY 4.1

Draw an image of Abel taking care of his flock of sheep.

ACTIVITY 4.2
Color this picture.

61

ACTIVITY 4.3

Read Genesis 4:25. Fill in the blanks to know how God's promised seed was fulfilled through Adam and Eve.

"And _____ knew his _____ again, and she bore a _____ and named him _____, 'For God has _____ another _____ for me instead of _____, whom _____ killed.'"

Note to teacher: *For this activity, please use the New King James Version.*

SAVED BY WATER

LESSON 5

Scripture: Genesis 6-9

Memory Verse: "But as the days of Noah were, so also will the coming of the Son of Man be." (Matthew 24:37)

Lesson Truth: The world is saved by water, when God saved Noah and his family.

LESSON

The whole earth was covered with water. All the people on the earth drowned except one family. That family was the family of Noah. Why did God destroy almost all the people on the earth? God destroyed them because they were so sinful. God's promise to Adam and Eve could never come from sinful people. So, He decided to save one faithful family. This family would one day have the Savior who would crush Satan's head.

God saved Noah and his family in a big boat. This boat was called an ark. God told Noah to build the ark. Noah's neighbors made fun of him when he built the ark. They did not think it would rain enough to cover the whole earth. Noah believed God. He built the ark anyway. One day God told Noah and his family to go into the ark. He also brought animals to Noah to put into the ark. Then the rains came and the oceans overflowed. Even the high mountains were covered with water (Show T.A. 5.1). Everyone drowned except Noah and his family. All the animals also drowned except the ones in the ark with Noah.

LESSON (Continued)

After the flood the earth finally dried. Noah and his family left the ark. Noah was thankful that God saved him. He made an altar and sacrificed to God. God liked his sacrifice. God promised Noah He would never send another big flood to destroy the whole earth. God said He would put the rainbow in the clouds so He would remember His promise about a flood (Show T.A. 5.2).

Noah believed God, but he was also a sinner. One day he became drunk. When he was drunk he lay in his tent naked. His youngest son, Ham, did not honor him. But his sons, Shem and Japheth, did honor him and covered him. Later, Noah woke from his drunkenness. He then talked like a prophet. He said Ham's son Canaan would be a slave. He said Shem would be blessed. The Savior would come from the family of Shem.

REVIEW QUESTIONS

Read these sentences to the students and ask them to say the correct answer.

1. God sent (a flood - a fire) to destroy the world.

2. God saved (Noah - his wife - his sons - his sons wives) in the ark.

3. God set (the dark clouds - the rainbow) as a sign He would not destroy the earth with a flood again.

4. Noah spoke as a prophet saying (Shem would be blessed - Canaan would be blessed).

ACTIVITIES

To recap this lesson, do Activity 5.1. In case you still have enough time in your class, do Activities 5.2 and 5.3.

TEACHING AIDS & ACTIVITIES

These teaching aids and activities are designed to help you convey and review the Lesson. If you need to scan and reprint any activity sheet for your class, cut along these cutting lines.

"And God said to Noah, 'The end of all flesh has come before Me, for the earth is filled with violence through them; and behold, I will destroy them with the earth.'"

Genesis 6:13

TEACHING AID 5.1
God saved Noah and his family in a big boat.

"And God said: 'This is the sign of the covenant which I make between Me and you, and every living creature that is with you, for perpetual generations: I set My rainbow in the cloud, and it shall be for the sign of the covenant between Me and the earth.'"

Genesis 9:12-13

TEACHING AID 5.2

God made the rainbow as a promise to Noah.

ACTIVITY 5.1

Color the rainbow using the number code.

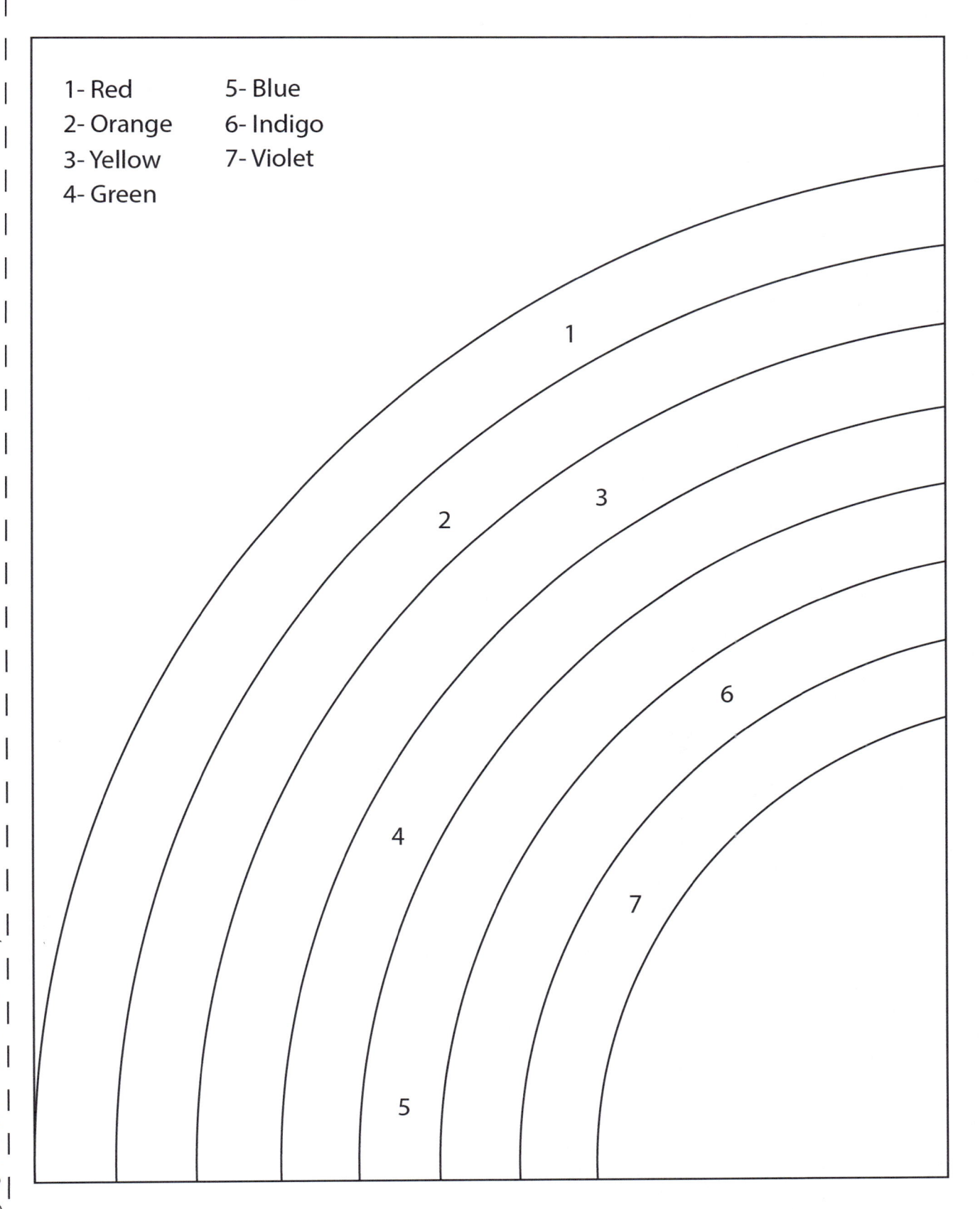

1- Red
2- Orange
3- Yellow
4- Green
5- Blue
6- Indigo
7- Violet

ACTIVITY 5.2
Color this picture.

ACTIVITY 5.3

Read Genesis 9:14-15. Fill in the blanks to know what is God's message behind every rainbow.

"It shall be, _____ I bring a _____ over the _____, that the _____ shall be _____ in the cloud; and I will _____ my _____ which is between Me and you and every _____ creature of all flesh; the _____ shall never again become a _____ to _____ all flesh."

Note to teacher: *For this activity, please use the New King James Version.*

THE EMERGENCE OF DISTINCT PEOPLES

LESSON 6

Scripture: Genesis 11:1-9

Memory Verse: "Behold how good and how pleasant it is for brethren to dwell together in unity." (Psalm 133:1)

Lesson Truth: Outward unity is torn down to make room for true unity in Christ.

LESSON

In time Noah's children moved to a plain called Shinar. At Shinar they became afraid. They did not want to become separated. They decided to build a city and a tower. "A huge tower will protect us," they thought. They forgot that only God can protect us. God wanted them to populate the whole earth.

God saw what the people were doing. He did not like to have them trust in a huge tower and city. He wanted them to trust in God. So, God decided to stop them from building. He gave each of these people a different language to speak. All these different languages were called Babel.

At Babel God showed how much He loves His people. He would not let them trust in a tower. He wanted them to trust in a Redeemer.

LESSON (Continued)

The people could not understand each other. They moved to different parts of the world. God made them into different people. They spoke different languages. No matter what their language, they needed love. God showed them how to become one again. A tower could not help them become one. They could become one by trusting in Jesus.

Boys and girls are still tempted. They are tempted to trust themselves. They are tempted, just like the people at Babel. Remember to trust only in Jesus. Trust in Jesus can help you be one with all people.

REVIEW QUESTIONS

Read these sentences to the students and ask them to say the correct answer.

1. The people of the earth lived on the plain of (Babel - Shinar - Ararat).

2. The people disobeyed God by building a (church - school - tower)

3. The Bible says, God (listened - came down - spoke).

4. God stopped their building by confusing their (language - tools - streets).

5. Because of this confusion the place was called (Shinar - Babel - Ararat).

ACTIVITIES

To recap this lesson, do Activity 6.1. In case you still have enough time in your class, do Activities 6.2 and 6.3.

TEACHING AIDS & ACTIVITIES

These teaching aids and activities are designed to help you convey and review the Lesson. If you need to scan and reprint any activity sheet for your class, cut along these cutting lines.

"Therefore its name is called Babel, because there the Lord confused the language of all the earth; and from there the Lord scattered them abroad over the face of all the earth."

Genesis 11:9

TEACHING AID 6.1
God made the the people speak different languages.

83

ACTIVITY 6.1

Read Genesis 11:7-8. Fill in the blanks to know what God did to the people of Babel.

"'_____, let Us go _____ and there _____ their _____, that they ____ not understand one another's _____.' So the Lord scattered them _____ from there over the face of all the _____, and they ceased building the ____."

Note to teacher: *For this activity, please use the New King James Version.*

ACTIVITY 6.2

Help the people of Shinar find the right path. Unscrambe these letters and write the word on the boxes below to reveal what God wants.

R E M E D E E R

God wants the people to trust in the

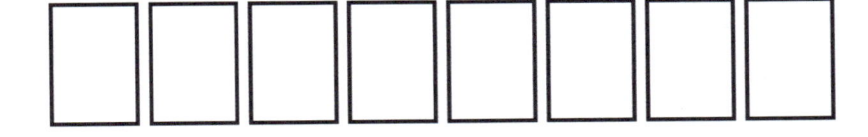

☐☐☐☐☐☐☐

87

ACTIVITY 6.3

Color this picture.

BLESSED IN THE ONE

LESSON 7

Scripture: Genesis 12

Memory Verse: "And in you all the families of the earth shall be blessed." (Genesis 12:3b)

Lesson Truth: God chose one through whom He would bless everyone.

LESSON

Today our story is about a man called Abram. God later changed his name to Abraham. God said he was to be the father of great nations. God had not talked to anyone in the world for a long time. Ever since the great flood God had been silent. In our story today we learn that God appeared to Abram. God told Abram that he and Sarai would have a son. He told Abram the children of this son would grow into a great nation (See T.A. 7.1). Then God told Abram something even more wonderful. He said that from this great nation He was going to send a Redeemer. A Redeemer is someone who can save us from our sins. Do you know who this Redeemer is?

God told Abram about the Redeemer. God then asked Abram to do some very hard things. He asked Abram to leave his family. The Lord also asked Abram to go to a new place to live. Isn't it wonderful that Abram obeyed God? He did what God wanted him to do. He left his family and went to a new place to live. He obeyed because God worked in his heart.

LESSON (Continued)

Isn't it sad that Abram did not always trust God to take care of him? One day he went to Egypt to find food. When he was in Egypt, he became afraid. He was afraid the people in Egypt would kill him and take his wife. So, he told Sarai to lie. He told Sarai to say that she was his sister. Sure enough, the Pharaoh in Egypt did try to take Sarai. But God could never let that happen. Sarai was to be the mother of the great nation God promised to Abram. Sarai was going to be the mother of the Redeemer.

REVIEW QUESTIONS

Read these sentences to the students and ask them to say the correct answer.

1. God asked Abram to leave his (family - country).

2. Abram's wife was (Sarai - Rebecca - Rachel).

3. God promised Abram He would become a (great army - great nation).

4. Abram told Sarai (to pray - to lie) when he was in Egypt.

5. God promised Abram that a (Pharaoh - Redeemer) would come from his children.

ACTIVITIES

To recap this lesson, do Activity 7.1. In case you still have enough time in your class, do Activities 7.2 and 7.3.

TEACHING AIDS & ACTIVITIES

These teaching aids and activities are designed to help you convey and review the Lesson. If you need to scan and reprint any activity sheet for your class, cut along these cutting lines.

"Now the Lord had said to Abram:

'Get out of your country,
From your family
And from your father's house,
To a land that I will show you.
I will make you a great nation;
I will bless you
And make your name great;
And you shall be a blessing.
I will bless those who bless you,
And I will curse him who curses you;
And in you all the families of the earth
shall be blessed.'"

Genesis 12:1-3

TEACHING AID 7.1
God calls Abram.

95

ACTIVITY 7.1

Write the correct letters in each box to complete the message.

TH☐N T☐E ☐O☐D A☐PE☐RE☐ T☐ A☐RA☐ A☐D S☐I☐, "☐O Y☐U☐ ☐ES☐EN☐A☐TS I W☐LL GI☐E THIS L☐N☐." A☐D T☐E☐E HE ☐UI☐T A☐ A☐TA☐ TO T☐E L☐R☐, ☐HO HA☐ AP☐E☐R☐D ☐O ☐IM.

GE☐E☐I☐ 12:7

ACTIVITY 7.2
Color this picture.

ACTIVITY 7.3

Draw Abram and Sarai, with family and servants, crossing a dry desert.

CHRIST ALONE

LESSON 8

Scripture: Genesis 13

Memory Verse: "And if you are Christ's, then you are Abraham's seed..." (Galatians 3:29a)

Lesson Truth: The blessings of God come through Jesus.

LESSON

Abram took his wife, Sarai, and his nephew, Lot, and moved to a new country. He obeyed God. He lived separate from his own family. Our story today tells us that God wanted Abram to be even more separate. He wanted Abram to be separate from Lot. God wanted Abram to be a picture of what Jesus would be. Jesus was separate from everything on the earth. How would Abram separate from Lot?

Both Abram and Lot had a lot of cattle and sheep. They were rich. There wasn't enough grass for all their flocks and herds. Abram did not want to quarrel with Lot. He said to Lot, "Please separate from me, if you take the left then I will go to the right; or if you go to the right then I will go to the left." Abram was very generous. He let Lot choose first. This was the way God helped Abram become all the way separate.

Lot chose the beautiful valley of the Jordan River (Show T.A. 8.1). This was a bad choice for Lot. It was bad because there were two very wicked cities in that valley. Lot set up his tent near Sodom.

LESSON (Continued)

Lot was no longer with Abram. Now God came to Abram. God gave Abram His rich promises. He had given these promises to Abram before. He told Abram he would become a great nation. This promise meant that God would make a special son come from Abram. This special son of Abram is Jesus.

REVIEW QUESTIONS

Read these sentences to the students and ask them to say the correct answer.

1. Abram moved to Canaan with his nephew (Isaac - Lot).

2. Abram took his wife (Sarai - Rebecca) to Canaan.

3. God wanted Abram and Lot to be (together - separate).

4. Lot chose to live near the city of (Sodom - Jerusalem).

5. The promised son of Abram is (Jacob - Jesus).

ACTIVITIES

To recap this lesson, do Activity 8.1. In case you still have enough time in your class, do Activities 8.2 and 8.3.

TEACHING AIDS & ACTIVITIES

These teaching aids and activities are designed to help you convey and review the Lesson. If you need to scan and reprint any activity sheet for your class, cut along these cutting lines.

"So Abram said to Lot, 'Please let there be no strife between you and me, and between my herdsmen and your herdsmen; for we are brethren.
Is not the whole land before you?
Please separate from me. If you take the left, then I will go to the right;
or, if you go to the right, then I will go to the left.'"

Genesis 13:8

TEACHING AID 8.1
Abram parts ways with his nephew Lot.

ACTIVITY 8.1

Color this picture.

ACTIVITY 8.2

Abram and Lot have lots of sheep. Check the mark on each sheep and count how many belong to Abram and how many is for Lot. Write your answer below.

Abram _____   Lot _____

ACTIVITY 8.3

Read Genesis 13:14-16. Fill in the blanks to know God's message to Abram after he and his family separated from Lot.

"...Lift your _____ now and look from the _____ where you are... for all the _____ which you see I _____ to you and your _____ forever. And I will make your _____ as the _____ of the _____; so that if a _____ could _____ the dust of the _____, then your _____ also could be _____."

Note to teacher: *For this activity, please use the New King James Version.*

BLESSED BY THE GREATER

LESSON 9

Scripture: Genesis 14

Memory Verse: "And he blessed him and said: Blessed be Abram of God most High…" (Genesis 14:19a)

Lesson Truth: Abram is blessed by someone greater than himself.

LESSON

Two important things happened in Abram's life. First, he won a battle against the king of Elam. Second, he met the priest of God Most High. Today we will learn about these two important things.

Four kings decided to fight their neighbors. One of the neighbors was the king of Sodom. Remember, Lot lived at Sodom. The kings attacked Sodom and other towns. They took their possessions. Lot was captured. Lot's family was also captured. This made Abram feel very bad. Lot was Abram's nephew.

Abram decided to rescue Lot. God was with Abram. He defeated the kings who had Lot. He captured the possessions. He also rescued Lot and his family. Abram brought the possessions back to the king of Sodom. He also brought back Lot and his family. The king of Sodom wanted to honor Abram. He wanted to give Abram all the captured possessions.

LESSON (Continued)

Abram did not take the possessions. He said, "God helped me win the battle. I did not win the battle myself. God gave me everything I own. The possessions from the battle did not make me rich. God made me rich."

Then a wonderful thing happened. The priest of God Most High met Abram. This priest blessed Abram (Show T.A. 9.1). He said God made you win the battle against your enemies. Do you know what Abram did? He gave this priest a tenth of everything. Abram now knew his blessings came from God. He knew his children would be blessed by our Lord Jesus Christ.

REVIEW QUESTIONS

Read these sentences to the students and ask them to say the correct answer.

1. Abram went to battle to rescue (Lot - Jacob) his nephew.

2. Abram captured the (priest - possessions) when he defeated the kings.

3. Abram said (God - the king of Sodom) made him rich.

4. Abram was blessed by (the king - the priest of God Most High).

5. Abram's children will be blessed by (our Lord Jesus Christ - the king).

ACTIVITIES

To recap this lesson, do Activity 9.1. In case you still have enough time in your class, do Activities 9.2 and 9.3.

TEACHING AIDS & ACTIVITIES

These teaching aids and activities are designed to help you convey and review the Lesson. If you need to scan and reprint any activity sheet for your class, cut along these cutting lines.

"Then Melchizedek king of Salem brought out bread and wine; he was the priest of God Most High.

And he blessed him and said:

'Blessed be Abram of God Most High,
Possessor of heaven and earth;
And blessed be God Most High,
Who has delivered your enemies into your hand.'

And he gave him a tithe of all."

Genesis 14:18-20

TEACHING AID 9.1
Melchizedek blesses Abram.

ACTIVITY 9.1

Decipher what Melchizedek said to Abram using this code.

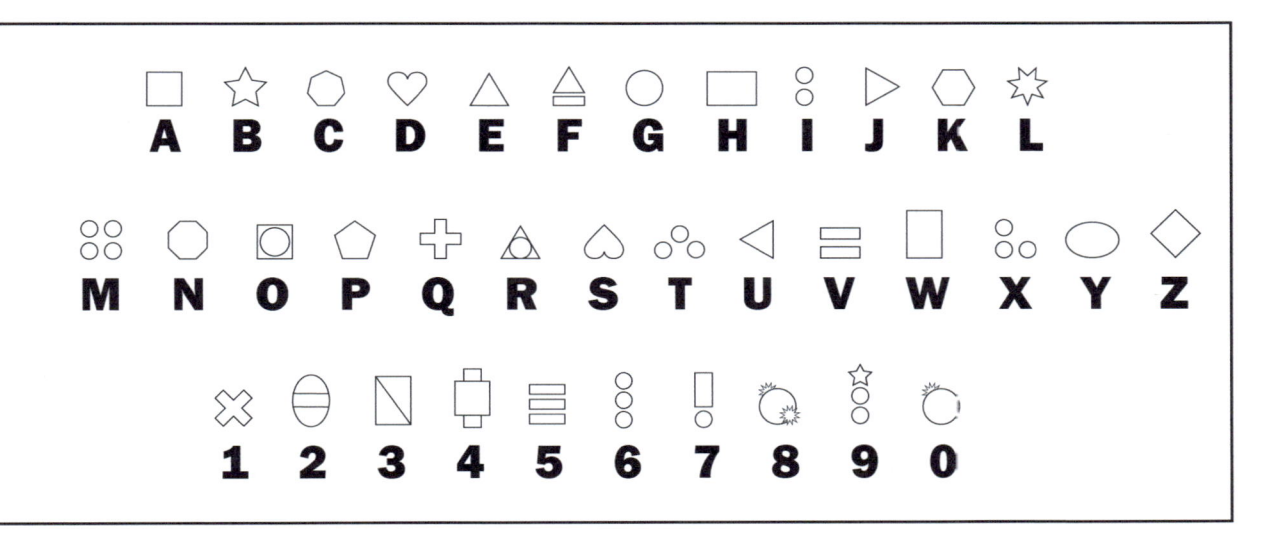

ACTIVITY 9.2

Read Genesis 14:14. Fill in the blanks to know what Abram did when he learned Lot and his family were taken captive.

"Now when _____ heard that his _____ was taken _____, he _____ his _____ hundred and _____ trained _____ who were _____ in his own _____, and went in _____ as far as Dan."

Note to teacher: *For this activity, please use the New King James Version.*

ACTIVITY 9.3
Color this picture.

THE LORD IN THE COVENANT

LESSON 10

Scripture: Genesis 15

Memory Verse: "Just as Abraham 'believed God and it was accounted to him for righteousness.'" (Galatians 3:6)

Lesson Truth: Jesus tells us He is the one who will keep the promises made to Abram and all believers.

LESSON

Have you ever made a promise to your mom or dad? Did you keep your promise? One day God made a promise to Abram. He gave Abram a sign that meant He would keep His promise. Today we will learn about God's promise to Abram. We will also learn how God showed Abram He would keep His promise.

God told Abram he would have many children. He told Abram that one of his children would bless all the nations. Abram was afraid this would not happen. He was afraid because he did not have any children at all. Then God came to Abram. God said to Abram, "Do not be afraid." He showed Abram all the stars in the sky. He told Abram his children would be as many as the stars. The Bible says Abram believed God.

God then gave Abram another promise. He promised the land of Canaan to Abram's children. Abram asked God, "How do I know your promise is true?" God told Abram He would show him a special sign. This sign meant that a promise was really, really true.

LESSON (Continued)

God showed Abram a sign of animals cut in two. The one who promised passed between the animal parts (Show T.A. 10.1). This meant the promise was true. The promise must be kept. Only God passed between the animal parts. Abram knew God would keep His promise.

God told Abram his children would be servants. They would be servants four hundred years. It really happened. Abram's children were servants in Egypt four hundred years. Now we know God always keeps His promises.

REVIEW QUESTIONS

Read these sentences to the students and ask them to say the correct answer.

1. God promised Abram (many children - a castle).

2. God told Abram (do not cry - do not be afraid).

3. God promised Abram's children the land of (Canaan - Moab).

4. God told Abram his children would be (kings - servants) for 400 years.

5. (God - Abram) always keeps His promises.

ACTIVITIES

To recap this lesson, do Activity 10.1. In case you still have enough time in your class, do Activities 10.2 and 10.3.

TEACHING AIDS & ACTIVITIES

These teaching aids and activities are designed to help you convey and review the Lesson. If you need to scan and reprint any activity sheet for your class, cut along these cutting lines.

"And it came to pass, when the sun went down and it was dark, that behold, there appeared a smoking oven and a burning torch that passed between those pieces."

Genesis 15:17

TEACHING AID 10.1

God sends Abram a sign He will fulfill His promise.

131

ACTIVITY 10.1

Read Genesis 15:5-6. Fill in the blanks to know how God considered Abram as righteous.

"Then He _____ him outside and said, '_____ now toward _____, and _____ the _____ if you are _____ to _____ them.' And ___ said to him, 'So _____ your _____ be.' And he _____ in the _____, and He _____ it to _____ for righteousness."

Note to teacher: *For this activity, please use the New King James Version.*

ACTIVITY 10.2

Color this picture.

135

ACTIVITY 10.3

Circle the correct group of stars that matches the number.

5	☆☆☆	☆☆	☆☆☆☆☆
8	☆☆☆☆☆☆☆☆☆	☆☆☆☆☆☆☆☆	☆☆☆☆☆☆☆
1	☆	☆☆☆☆	☆☆☆☆
3	☆☆	☆☆☆☆☆☆	☆☆☆
6	☆☆☆☆☆☆	☆☆☆	☆☆
4	☆☆☆	☆☆☆☆☆☆	☆☆☆☆
7	☆☆☆	☆☆☆☆☆☆☆☆☆	☆☆☆☆☆☆☆☆

GOD HEARS

LESSON 11

Scripture: Genesis 16

Memory Verse: "My voice You shall hear in the morning, O Lord." (Psalm 5:3a)

Lesson Truth: God hears His children when they cry to Him.

LESSON

God takes care of His family. He took care of Hagar. Hagar was Sarai's maid. She was from Abram's house. So, God took care of her. Sarai wanted to have a child. God had not yet given her a child. Sarai thought, "I will get a child from Hagar, my maid." Abram thought this would work. But, this was not God's way.

Hagar was going to have a baby. She did not like Sarai, her mistress. Sarai wanted to have Hagar's baby. Hagar ran away. She ran into the wilderness. Hagar was very tired. She sat by a spring of water. The Angel of the Lord found her. The Angel said to Hagar, "You must go back to Sarai. The baby you will have, will become a great nation. You must name your baby, Ishmael." Ishmael means, the Lord hears.

Hagar obeyed the Angel. She went back to Sarai and Abram. Hagar's baby was born. Abram gave him the name, Ishmael. Abram knew this was the right name. He knew the name, Ishmael, means the Lord hears. The Lord did hear Hagar in the wilderness.

REVIEW QUESTIONS

Read these sentences to the students and ask them to say the correct answer.

1. Sarai's maidservant was (Hagar - Ruth).

2. Hagar ran away to (the city - the wilderness).

3. The Angel of the Lord talked to (Hagar - Sarai).

4. Abram named Hagar's son (Jacob - Ishmael).

5. The name, Ishmael, means (God Hears - Abram Hears).

ACTIVITIES

To recap this lesson, do Activity 11.1. In case you still have enough time in your class, do Activities 11.2 and 11.3.

TEACHING AIDS & ACTIVITIES

These teaching aids and activities are designed to help you convey and review the Lesson. If you need to scan and reprint any activity sheet for your class, cut along these cutting lines.

"And the Angel of the Lord said to her:

'Behold, you are with child,
And you shall bear a son.
You shall call his name Ishmael,
Because the Lord has heard your affliction.'"

Genesis 16:11

TEACHING AID 11.1
Hagar flees from Sarai.

ACTIVITY 11.1

Color this picture.

145

ACTIVITY 11.2

Find these words in the word grid below.

Hagar	Ishmael	Spring
Maid	Hears	Water
Baby	Angel	Care

Y	H	R	A	M	E	Q	Y	B	U
M	Y	A	R	E	M	I	Y	E	O
S	N	H	G	N	L	B	U	C	S
M	A	I	D	A	A	R	C	T	T
R	W	G	M	B	R	R	W	Y	S
I	S	H	M	A	E	L	A	E	P
A	Y	E	J	I	L	V	T	E	R
N	U	A	Y	A	N	G	E	L	I
G	X	R	A	S	X	M	R	K	N
W	S	S	G	C	A	R	E	M	G

ACTIVITY 11.3

Draw Hagar in the wilderness resting under a shrub.

GOD THE ALMIGHTY

LESSON 12

Scripture: Genesis 17

Memory Verse: "I am Almighty God; walk before Me and be blameless." (Genesis 17:1b)

Lesson Truth: God told Abraham that He is Almighty.

LESSON

God gave promises to Abram. God promised that Abram would have children. He promised that all the nations would be blessed by Abram's children. Abram did not have a godly son. Abram and Sarai were old. How could God keep His Promises, Abram wondered?

God appeared to Abram. God said, "I am Almighty God. I can do all things. I can give old people a child. I can give you and Sarai a child. I promised you would have children. I keep my promises."

"Abram, I will help you to trust me. I will give you a new name. Your new name will be Abraham. Abraham means you will be the father of many nations. I will give Sarai a new name. Her new name will be Sarah. Sarah means she shall be the mother of nations. Sarah means kings and peoples will come from her."

Now Abraham knew God would keep His promises. He and Sarah would have a child. Even though they were old, God would give them a child. God is Almighty. God can do everything.

REVIEW QUESTIONS

Read these sentences to the students and ask them to say the correct answer.

1. Almighty God appeared to (Abram – Isaac).

2. God changed Abram's name to (Ishmael – Abraham).

3. God changed Sarai's name to (Sarah – Hagar).

4. Abraham means (Father of Nations – Father of Israel).

5. Sarah means (Mother of Ishmael – Mother of Nations).

ACTIVITIES

To recap this lesson, do Activity 12.1. In case you still have enough time in your class, do Activities 12.2 and 12.3.

TEACHING AIDS & ACTIVITIES

These teaching aids and activities are designed to help you convey and review the Lesson. If you need to scan and reprint any activity sheet for your class, cut along these cutting lines.

"When Abram was ninety-nine years old, the Lord appeared to him and said, 'I am God Almighty; walk before me faithfully and be blameless.'"

Genesis 17:11

TEACHING AID 12.1

Abraham fell facedown before God.

ACTIVITY 12.1

Read Genesis 17:7 Fill in the blanks to know about the promise God gave to Abraham.

"And I will _____ My _____ between Me and ___ and your _____ after you in their generations, for an _____ covenant, to be ____ to you and your descendants _____ you."

Note to teacher: *For this activity, please use the New King James Version.*

ACTIVITY 12.2

Count the number of stars in the boxes and find its matching letters in the word code. Number 16, for example, is for the letter P. Then write the letters on the blank lines to know the meaning of Abraham's name.

A B C D E F G H I J K L M N O P Q R S
1 2 3 4 5 6 7 8 9 10 11 12 13 14 15 16 17 18 19

T U V W X Y Z
20 21 22 23 24 25 26

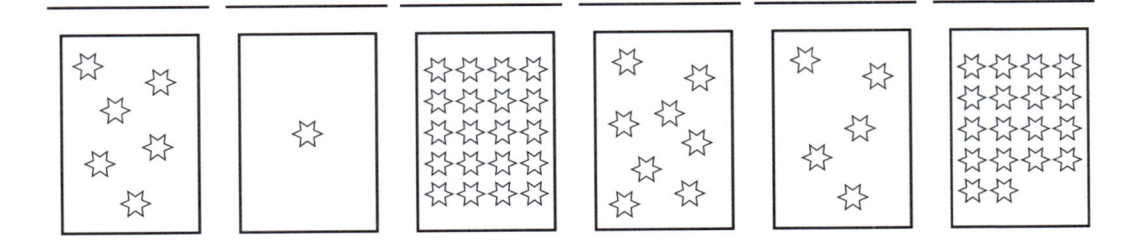

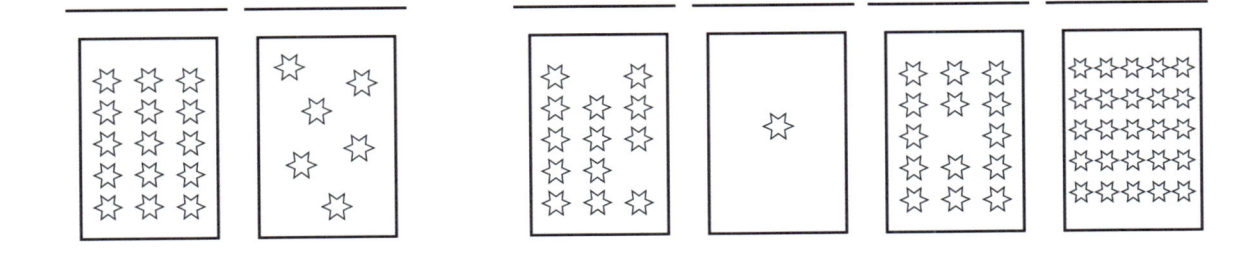

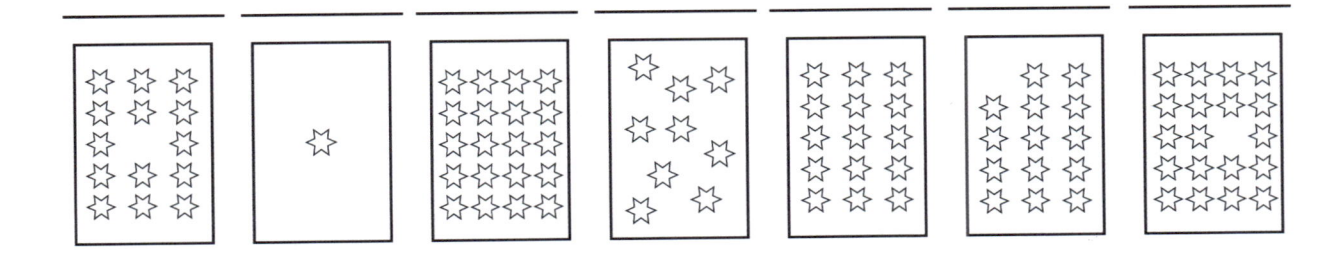

ACTIVITY 12.3

Color this picture.

ANSWER KEYS

ACTIVITY 1.2
Circle all the creatures God made on Day 5.

- (Eagle)
- Lakes
- Adam
- Pumpkin
- Angels
- (Goldfish)
- Hippo
- Birch
- (Whale Shark)
- (Lion)
- Oak
- (Hen)
- (Blue Jay)
- Scorpion
- Earthworm
- Eve

ACTIVITY 2.1
Read Genesis 2:15-17. Then fill in the blanks to know what God assigned to Adam and what He told him about the trees in the Garden.

"Then the **LORD God** took the man and **put him** in the **Garden** of **Eden** to **tend** and **keep** it. And the Lord God **commanded** the man, saying, 'Of **every tree** of the **garden** you may **freely** eat; but of **the tree** of the **knowledge** of **good** and **evil** you shall **not eat**, for in **the day** that you **eat** of it **you shall surely die**.'"

Note to teacher: For this activity, please use the New King James Version.

ACTIVITY 2.2
Answer these six sentences by writing the missing words on the blanks and on the squares below. Afterward, identify the word formed through the shaded squares to complete this sentence:

God placed Adam and Eve in the _____ of Eden.

1. _____ made the heavens and the earth.
2. God wanted _____ and Eve to take care of His beautiful garden.
3. God said Adam and Eve would be His special _____ if they would obey Him.
4. Adam and Eve could eat the fruit from all the trees in the garden except one in the _____ of the garden.
5. Sadly, Adam and _____ did not obey God.
6. Because Jesus obeyed God, Adam and Eve could once _____ be God's friends.

Crossword:
1. GOD
2. ADAM
3. FRIENDS
4. MIDDLE
5. EVE
6. AGAIN

ACTIVITY 3.2
Solve this maze to help Adam and Eve find their new home outside the Garden of Eden.

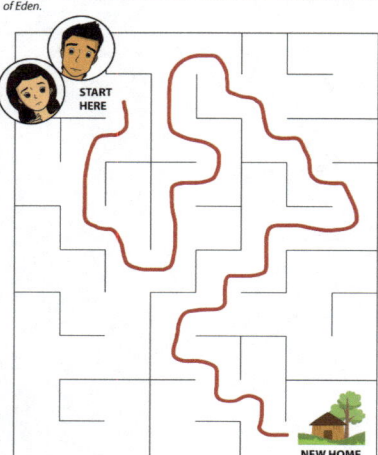

ACTIVITY 3.3
Color the letters below. Afterward, write each letter on the box that matches its assigned number to reveal what God gave to Adam and Eve after they sinned.

N(1) R(10) E(?) S(9) I(8) O(6) M(7) P(4) E(5) W(3)

NEW PROMISE
1 2 3 4 5 6 7 8 9 10

ACTIVITY 4.3
Read Genesis 4:25. Then fill in the blanks to know how God's promised seed was fulfilled through Adam and Eve.

"And **Adam** knew his **wife** again, and she bore a **son** and named him **Seth**, 'For God has **appointed** another **seed** for me instead of **Abel**, whom **Cain** killed.'"

Note to teacher: For this activity, please use the New King James Version.

ACTIVITY 5.3
Read Genesis 9:14-15. Then fill in the blanks to know what is God's message behind every rainbow.

"It shall be, **when** I bring a **cloud** over the **earth**, that the **rainbow** shall be **seen** in the cloud; and I will **remember** my **covenant** which is between Me and you and every **living** creature of all flesh; the **waters** shall never again become a **flood** to **destroy** all flesh."

Note to teacher: For this activity, please use the New King James Version.

ACTIVITY 6.1
Read Genesis 11:7-8. Then fill in the blanks to know what God did to the people of Babel.

"'**Come**, let Us go **down** and there **confuse** their **language**, that they **may** not understand one another's **speech**.' So the Lord scattered them **abroad** from there over the face of all the **earth**, and they ceased building the **city**."

Note to teacher: For this activity, please use the New King James Version.

ACTIVITY 6.2
Help the people of Shinar find the right path. Unscramble these letters and write the word on the boxes below to reveal what God wants.

R E D E E M E R

God wants the people to trust in the
REDEEMER

ACTIVITY 7.1
Write the correct letters in each box to complete the message.

THEN THE LORD APPEARED TO ABRAM AND SAID, "TO YOUR DESCENDANTS I WILL GIVE THIS LAND." AND THERE HE BUILT AN ALTAR TO THE LORD, WHO HAD APPEARED TO HIM.

GENESIS 12:7

ACTIVITY 8.2
Abram and Lot have lots of sheep. Check the mark on each sheep and count how many belong to Abram and how many is for Lot. Write your answer below.

Abram __12__   Lot __11__

ACTIVITY 8.3
Read Genesis 13:14-16. Then fill in the blanks to know what is God's message to Abram after he and his family separated from Lot.

"...Lift your __eyes__ now and look from the __place__ where you are... for all the __land__ which you see I __give__ to you and your __descendants__ forever. And I will make your __descendants__ as the __dust__ of the __earth__; so that if a __man__ could __number__ the dust of the __earth__, then your __descendants__ also could be __numbered__."

Note to teacher: *For this activity, please use the New King James Version.*

ACTIVITY 9.1
Decipher what Melchizedek said to Abram using this code.

BLESSED BE ABRAM OF GOD MOST HIGH, POSSESSOR OF HEAVEN AND EARTH; AND BLESSED BE GOD MOST HIGH, WHO HAS DELIVERED YOUR ENEMIES INTO YOUR HAND.

GENESIS 14:19-20

ACTIVITY 9.2
Read Genesis 14:14. Then fill in the blanks to know what Abram did when he learned Lot and his family were taken captive.

"Now when __Abram__ heard that his __brother__ was taken __captive__, he __armed__ his __three__ hundred and __eighteen__ trained __servants__ who were __born__ in his own __house__, and went in __pursuit__ as far as Dan."

ACTIVITY 10.1
Read Genesis 15:5-6. Then fill in the blanks to know how God considered Abram as righteous.

"Then He __brought__ him outside and said, '__Look__ now toward __heaven__, and __count__ the __stars__ if you are __able__ to __number__ them.' And __He__ said to him, 'So __shall__ your __descendants__ be.' And he __believed__ in the __LORD__, and He __accounted__ it to __him__ for righteousness."

Note to teacher: *For this activity, please use the New King James Version.*

ACTIVITY 10.3
Circle the correct group of stars that matches the number.

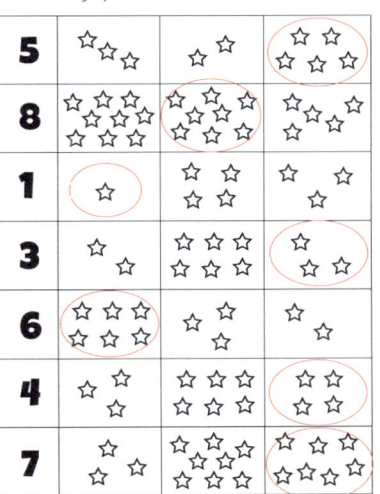

ACTIVITY 11.2
Find these words in the word grid below.

Hagar, Ishmael, Spring, Maid, Hears, Water, Baby, Angel, Care

ACTIVITY 12.1
Read Genesis 17:7 Then fill in the blanks to know about the promise God gave to Abraham.

"And I will __establish__ My __covenant__ between Me and __you__ and your __descendants__ after you in their generations, for an __everlasting__ covenant, to be __God__ to you and your descendants __after__ you."

Note to teacher: *For this activity, please use the New King James Version.*

165

ACTIVITY 12.1

Read Genesis 17:7 Then fill in the blanks to know about the promise God gave to Abraham.

"And I will __establish__ My __covenant__ between Me and __you__ and your __descendants__ after you in their generations, for an __everlasting__ covenant, to be __God__ to you and your descendants __after__ you."

Note to teacher: *For this activity, please use the New King James Version.*

ACTIVITY 12.2

Count the number of stars in the boxes and find its matching letters in the word code. Number 16, for example, is for the letter P. Then write the letters on the blank lines to know the meaning of Abraham's name.

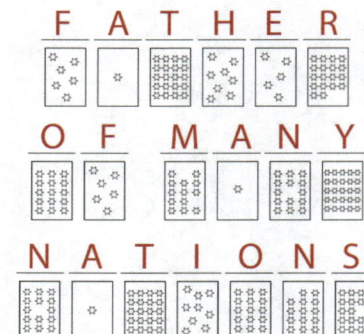

A B C D E F G H I J K L M N O P Q R S
1 2 3 4 5 6 7 8 9 10 11 12 13 14 15 16 17 18 19

T U V W X Y Z
20 21 22 23 24 25 26

FATHER

OF MANY

NATIONS

166

Made in the USA
Columbia, SC
23 August 2024